Crow Said No

written by Angela B. Haight
illustrated by Barbara Spurll

KAEDEN ❤ BOOKS™

Crow Said No
Copyright © 2015 Kaeden Corporation
Author: Angela B. Haight
Illustrator: Barbara Spurll

ISBN: 978-1-61181-903-8 *(TCA paperback)*
ISBN: 978-1-61181-639-6 *(eBook)*

Published by:
Kaeden Corporation
P.O. Box 16190
Rocky River, Ohio 44116
1-800-890-7323
www.kaeden.com

Printed in Guangzhou, China
NOR/1015/CA21501478

First edition 2015
Second edition 2015

 # CONTENTS

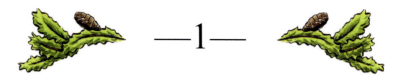

Crow Has a Visitor

Crow lived in a tall tree. One day a finch flew by his tree. "May I stop here?" she asked.

"No," said Crow. "This is my tree."

"I am tired," said Finch. "Please let me rest."

"Just a little while," said Crow.

"May I sing?" asked Finch.

"No," said Crow. "No singing."

"Why not?" asked Finch. "Your tree is so beautiful. It makes me feel like singing."

"Really?" said Crow. "Well, just one song."

"Tweet, tweet, tweet, tweet!" Finch twittered and trilled. "Did you like my song?" she asked.

"No," said Crow.

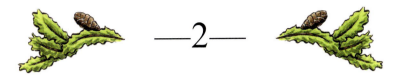

Night Is Coming

Finch looked around. "Night is coming," she said. "May I stay here?"

"No," said Crow. "No visitors."

"Where can I go?" asked Finch.

"Find another tree," said Crow.

Then Crow looked around too. It was almost dark.

"Oh, all right," he said. "Just one night."

"Thank you," Finch said.

Finch gathered twigs and grass. She made a small nest.

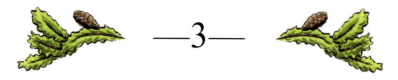

—3—

Just One More Night

"Good morning, Crow," Finch called the next morning. "I am still tired. May I stay one more night?"

"No," said Crow.

"Please?" said Finch. "This nest is so comfortable. I won't bother you at all."

Crow groaned. "All right," he said.
"One more night."

All day Finch flew back and forth. She put more twigs in the nest. She lined it with fresh grass.

"Now I can rest," she said.

Finch settled down for the night.

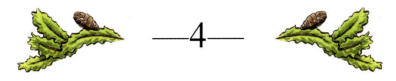

Finch's Surprise

When the sun rose, Crow heard twittering.

"Are you leaving?" he called.

"Not yet," Finch said. "I have a surprise. Come and see."

Three eggs lay in the nest.

"No, no, no!" said Crow. "No eggs!"

"This is my mate," Finch said.

"No, no, no," said Crow. "No more visitors."

"I'm sorry," said Finch. "I can't go now. I can't leave my eggs."

"Then *I* will go," said Crow.

"Why?" asked Finch. "Your tree is big. There is room for all of us."

"Do you think so?" asked Crow.

"Yes," said Finch. "We won't stay long."

19

"But it is *my* tree," said Crow.

"Of course," said Finch. "It is your tree. Please don't go."

"Oh, all right," said Crow.

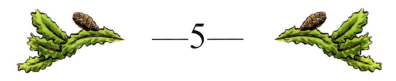

—5—
Another Visitor

A shadow passed over the tree.

"Hello, Cousin Crow!" someone called.

"Hey, Cousin Jay!" Crow said.
"It has been a long time since I have
seen you. Where have you been?"

"Here and there," said Jay. "How about
you?"

"Right here," said Crow. "I'm guarding my tree."

Jay looked around. "Is it going somewhere?" he asked.

"No, I've got visitors," said Crow.

"Visitors? You?" asked Jay.

"Take a look," said Crow.

Jay glided around the tree. "You've got trouble," he said. "Can I help?"

"How?" asked Crow.

Jay flapped his wings.

"I'll buzz the nest. I'll squawk and screech. I'll scare them away," said Jay.

"No," said Crow. "No scaring."

Jay clacked his beak.

"I'll eat them up. I love eggs," he said.

"No, no," said Crow. "No eating."

"Then I'll knock that nest right out of your tree," said Jay.

"No, no, no!" shouted Crow.
"Leave them alone."

Jay shrugged. "Then I can't help you," he said. "Wait until I tell the flock about your hotel."

"Please don't tell," said Crow. "It's not a hotel. They'll go soon."

Jay started to giggle. He laughed so hard he shook.

"See you later, alligator," he cackled.

"Stop!" shouted Crow. "Don't go!"

But Cousin Jay took off. "Ha, ha, ha!" he screeched. "Hotel Crow!
Ha, ha, ha!"

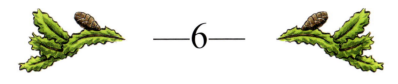

—6—

Waiting

Crow sat on top of the tree.

Finch sat on her eggs.

Finch's mate brought food to her.

Every day Crow asked, "Have the eggs hatched yet?"

"Not yet," Finch always said. "Soon, soon."

They waited and waited.

One morning Crow heard new noises.

"Cheep! Cheep! Cheep!"

"What's that?" he asked.

"The babies have hatched," Finch said. "Now watch them grow."

Day after day Crow watched.

The babies gobbled and gulped.

The babies chattered and chirped.

The babies fluttered and flapped.

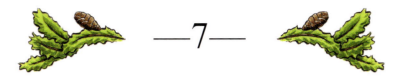

—7—

Time to Go

One day Finch said, "Thank you, Crow. You have been a kind friend. Now we can go."

"Go?" asked Crow. "Why?"

"The babies can fly," said Finch.

"So soon?" asked Crow.

"Yes," said Finch.

"Where will you go?" asked Crow.

"We will find another tree. This is your tree," said Finch.

"No," said Crow. "Don't go. This is our tree now."